minimalism & colour

Published in 2004 by
Conran Octopus Limited
part of Octopus Publishing Group
2–4 Heron Quays
London E14 4JP
www.conran-octopus.co.uk

First published in US in 2002 by HBI
an imprint of HarperCollins International
10 East 53rd Street, New York NY 10022-5229

Copyright © 2002 Atrium Group
Atrium Group
C/ Ganduxer, 112,1
08022 Barcelona
Spain

Publishing Director
Nacho Asensio

Editorial coordination and original texts
Patricia Bueno

Design and layout
Núria Sordé Orpinell

English Translation
Peter Miller / Simon Thornton

Production
Juanjo Rodríguez Novel

ISBN 1 84091 372 X

Printed in Spain

minimalism & colour

Architecture & Interiors & Furniture

conran OCTOPUS

contents

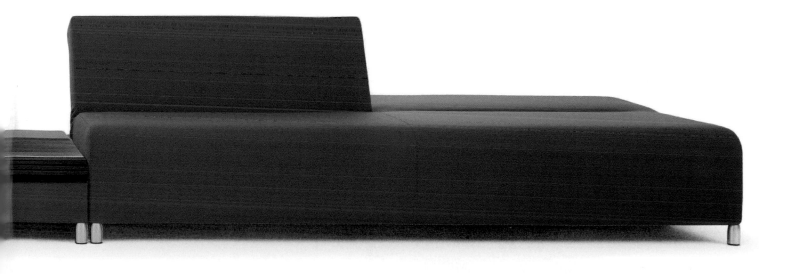

introduction

Minimalism, where interior decoration is concerned, cannot be looked at as a stylistic trend or fashion, but rather something which transcends these frontiers, and becomes an authentic philosophy of life. It seeks the creation of a new society, one anchored only to the essential and which therefore moves away from materialistic eagerness.

Although the means employed are relatively new –minimalism has been exercising its influence on the concept of domestic space for a little more than a decade– the search for a lifestyle based on simplicity goes back a long way. Its roots are found beyond the theories and geometric shapes of Bauhaus and, beyond the "less is more" dictum coined by Mies van der Rohe; rather, the rigorous renunciation of the monastic cells from the Middle Ages, the Japanese "wabi-sabi" aesthetic of voluntary poverty, and the spirituality of Zen philosophy, with its reverence for emptiness, are some of the sources of inspiration.

From this perspective, the application of colour in a minimalist environment is no longer a paradoxical or apparently contradictory presence, but rather it becomes a means of expression and contrast, capable of communicating a great deal with a simple brush stroke. On the other hand, this vision reflects an erosion of the strictest minimalism, which preaches total adhesion to the colour white, the elimination of any kind of ornamentation, and an evolution towards more flexible forms, which permit greater freedom for the individual. Living in a minimalist ambience is an option which implies an attempt at renunciation and containment, of liberation from all useless things, and of a reduction to basic elements. This means that, to achieve a working minimalist home, the capacity to live with the minimum must be the first step. Thus, starting out with the goal of reduction, the spatial and material qualities of the house are enhanced, creating an atmosphere which has a direct bearing on the sensory experience. Colour contributes to the enrichment of this experience generated in emptiness, imbuing meaning to this way of life.

"The suppression of decoration is
necessary to regulate passion."

Adolf Loos

Interiors & Minimalism: Influences

Minimalism & the Modern Movement

In order to precisely define minimalism, it is necessary to study its origins in the Modern Movement, identified with functionalism, which was developed in Europe after the First World War. This movement came about as architects, designers, and craftsmen, united by a spirit of innovation, reacted against the dominance of historicism, which had been present in previous styles. The result was a radical change in the cultural and aesthetic sensitivity of society, particularly evident in art and literature.

Of a more ideological than aesthetic nature, the representatives of the Modern Movement, especially those of the Bauhaus school, understood design as a means of improving society, from changing the conceptions of building construction to the creation of a simple chair.

■

"There are two ways to achieve joy and
happiness. One way is to highlight the
sensual beauty of everything that
surrounds us. The other is to eliminate
anything that might cast a shadow over it."

Ou Baholyodhin

In this sense, one can observe the influence of the Arts and Crafts movement, which developed in the United States and Great Britain between the end of the nineteenth century and the beginning of the twentieth. The objective of introducing social and aesthetic reforms based on the restoration of craftsmanship and on simple designs made from natural materials gave rise to the creation of furniture that led to the geometric style of the De Stijl group and the Bauhaus school, founded by Walter Gropius in 1919. In the United States, the movement focused on a predominant theme: the democratic interest in ennobling the virtues of honesty and simplicity in the design of objects intended for daily use. From this relation arose three key concepts that we find in the basis of modern-day minimalist interiors: geometry, simplicity and honesty.

Within minimalist decoration, we can observe shapes that are reminiscent of the De Stijl group, developed between 1917 and 1928, which produced some of the most representative designs of the twentieth century, such as the geometric paintings of Piet Mondrian and the revolutionary furniture of Gerrit Rietveld. Its connection with contemporary minimalist style can be observed in the principal constants of De Stijl: the use of rectangles and squares in flat planes of bold primary colours, together with black, gray and white, all carefully orchestrated with straight lines.

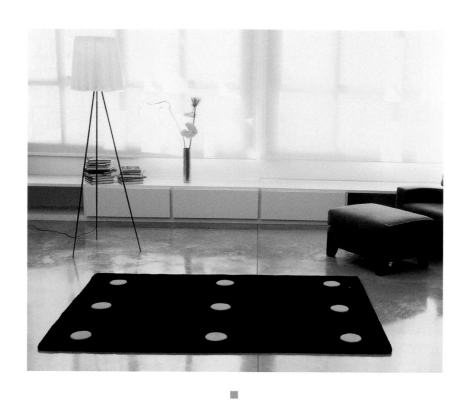

"A place becomes your home when
you are sincere."

Ou Baholyodhin

As far as the aesthetic premises established by Bauhaus are concerned, apart from the already mentioned concepts of geometry, simplicity and honesty, one can also extract further influences that have been absorbed by minimalism: universality, direct expression, standardization, economy and the application of new technologies. However, the contribution of the Bauhaus school with regard to the creation of a new domestic environment does not only take shape today through its influence on minimalism but also through the practical innovations that were introduced, namely the marriage of engineering with craftsmanship. These innovations have profoundly affected current industrial design and have come to form part of our lives. As Frank Whitford comments in his book *Bauhaus,* "Everyone sitting on a chair with a tubular steel frame, using an adjustable reading lamp, or living in a house partly or entirely constructed from prefabricated elements is benefiting from a revolution in design largely brought about by the Bauhaus."

The introduction of colour accents
within a world of white recalls the fact
that white light is the origin of the entire
spectrum of colours.

At the base of this revolution can be found one of the principal Bauhaus proposals, established by Gropius, "to make modern artists become familiar with science and economy by uniting creative imagination with a practical knowledge of craftsmanship, and thus to develop a new sense of functional design." This concept took shape through three principal objectives: primarily, to encourage individual craftsmen in different fields to work together and combine their skills; secondarily, to elevate the status of crafts (chairs, lamps, teapots, etc.) to the same level enjoyed by fine arts (painting, sculpture, etc.) by affirming that a house and the utensils found within have to sensibly relate to each other; and finally, to maintain contact with the leaders of industry in order to sell the craftsmen's work and to gain independence from government support.

One of the most prominent representatives of the Bauhaus school and its director between 1930 and 1933, Ludwig Mies van der Rohe, is fundamental to the very genesis of minimalism. Considered to be the most representative minimalist architect of the twentieth century, his notion of universal space turned empty spaces into a cornerstone of his work. For interiors, he proposed molding empty spaces, dilating them until he removed the barriers between interior and exterior. To do this, he freed the interior space of traditional structures and enclosures, like columns and walls, which had always been used to create different rooms. This new conception of space, full of significant emptiness, reminds us of present day lofts, the paradigm of a new lifestyle based on freedom and the search for simple forms.

"But, after all, the aim of art is to create space – space which is not occupied by decoration or illustration, space within which the subjects of painting can live."

Frank Stella, minimalist artist

Of all Mies van der Rohe's work, the Barcelona German Pavilion, built in 1929 for the Universal Exhibition and considered by many critics to be the quintessence of spatial abstraction in architecture, is a perfect example of the parallels between his architecture and today's minimalist interiors. In both cases, the empty space takes on meaning through the individual experience of each person. When either visiting the pavilion or when entering a minimalist home, moving around the space transforms the apparent severity and austerity of these spaces into an eloquent composition, giving the atmosphere an indescribable spirituality.

In 1933, when the Nazi majority came to power, the Bauhaus school was closed and the majority of its leaders, including Gropius and Mies van der Rohe, immigrated to the United States. The American adaptation of Bauhaus architecture took on the name of International Style, developing, along with its technological and ideological contributions, skyscraper architecture, which consequently became a symbol of capitalism. The premise of this style was the development of an impeccable architecture based on pure geometric forms. Thus, purity, smooth flat surfaces, and simplicity attained through the removal of ornamentation are some of the concepts associated with these projects, which include buildings designed by Le Corbusier, one of the most influential architects of the twentieth century. The Seagram Building in New York, built in bronze and glass and designed by Mies van der Rohe in collaboration with Philip Johnson, is one of the best-known examples of this style.

"Each moment eclipses the one before.
Whatever happens, this is the present.
Build your house here."

modern Zen meditation

The practitioners of the new International Style architecture aimed to create universal structures with a powerful presence that portray lightness, using technology that permits the design of open plans and that increase the availability of natural light. Most contemporary architecture falls within these formal constants.

Minimalism & Art

The term minimalism was applied for the first time to an artistic movement developed at the end of the 1960s in the United States as a reaction against the subjectivity of abstract expressionism and against the visual greed of the society of that era. For this reason, minimalist works of art are reduced to a minimum number of colours, values, shapes, lines and textures. The exponents of this style embarked on a quest for the essential, eliminating from the work of art any evidence whatsoever of the artist's hand, fleeing from the notion of art as a means of personal expression, and rejecting representation or symbolization of any type of object or experience.

■

"At the beginning of the last century,
decoration was applied to everything,
from a beer stein to a door handle. In
this, Adolf Loos perceived a mixture of
reality and fantasy, which was highly
damaging to both of them. The principles
of design of objects for use should be
solely objective and determined by the
functions the object must fulfill."

A. Janik and S. Toulmin

Minimalist art seeks to reference art itself, presenting, rather than repre-
senting. Through its use of geometry, clarity, precision, and non-relational
organization of the parts, minimalist art places the emphasis on the real,
the material, the here and now. Frank Stella, one of its advocates, offers an
easy summary of the movement's ideology referring to one of his paintings:
"What you see is what you see."

The extension of the minimalist label to other forms of expression, such
as music, cinema, dance, literature and architecture, makes it difficult to
precisely define the movement. In general terms that might allow us to cov-
er all the arts, the minimalist style is characterized by severity of means, clarity of form, and simplicity of structure and texture.

Colour plays a vital role in the world
in which we live. When used correctly,
it can save on energy consumption.
When used erroneously, it can contribute
to global pollution.

Minimalist artists use silence, repetition and the exposure of the medium to induce a kind of meditational receptivity in the spectator. Silence can be understood as space: quietness, emptiness, essence and absence create a space that induces passive meditation. In the visual arts, space is frequently used, whether through the absence of definite images on a blank canvas or through the air surrounding a sculpture in a museum. In this way, musicians, such as John Cage or Karlheinz, or plastic artists, such as Frank Stella, Dan Flavin or Donald Judd, manage to introduce into the audience's mind something that is almost impossible to achieve in an urban environment: silence, space and absence. As far as the method of repetition is concerned, it consists of the recurrence of similar patterns, as in the repetition of lines, with the same objective as the use of silence: to create a meditative space that does not fall into the trap of provoking boredom. Finally, the exposure of the medium supposes minimal technical complexity, so that the artist simplifies the artistic method to such an extent that he reveals to the audience what is hidden behind "art." This method was applied to sculpture; works of art were taken down from their pedestals and placed directly on the floor of the exhibition hall so that spectators could walk around the piece with complete freedom. In this way, a new relationship between the artist and the audience was forged, in which the space that the sculpture occupied also became important, changing the way in which art is contemplated. As a result of this change, sculpture acquired a new state of independence.

■

"A project for a piece of furniture
implies the design of an environment,
where the use of this piece, its position
and its relationship with the other pieces
of furniture are the means used to
participate in the daily rituals of
domestic behavior."

Antonio Citterio

The minimalist movement broke other artistic conventions that were present at the time. For example, the sculptor Donald Judd deliberately challenged the traditional artistic convention of originality by using industrial processes and materials such as steel, concrete and plywood to create large and hollow minimalist sculptures. Most of these sculptures took in the form of boxes which he arranged in repeated simple geometric forms.

When one observes a relatively purist minimalist interior, the parallels between the interior and the artistic movement become obvious. One might even claim that what began in the United States in the 1960's as an artistic movement has transformed into a way of life that has arguably become the best example of life imitating art.

Consequently, we can conclude that some proposals put forward by minimalist artists lie at the root of the conception of minimalist interiors. On the one hand, in its idealistic aspect, the objective of neutralizing the values of a highly industrialized society remains. On the other hand, this objective is related to its practical application: the rejection of all that is narrative, symbolic, mimetic, or fetishistic, so that significance is constructed by the spectator's own perception. Silence, emptiness, quietness, space, absence, methodical simplification, independence with respect to tradition, geometry, and the importance of texture, qualities inherent in minimalist works of art, all find continuity in this new style of living.

The concept of "form follows
function" represents the desire
of the Modern Movement to replace
unnecessary objects with
indispensable forms.

The connection between a work of art and a minimalist interior is clear: the essence of minimalism forces us to look into ourselves in order to discover why a particular shape or colour evokes such powerful emotions, independent of any rational context or secondary associations. In other words, both minimalist art and interiors are able to evoke emotion and aesthetic pleasure derived from their manifesto of clarity and perfect order. Perhaps the success of minimalism, in both art and decoration, results from its skill at invoking the most universal passions through the austerity of the media used, challenging the march of time.

Minimalism & Zen

Clear precedents for Western minimalist interiors can be observed in certain concepts of some oriental philosophies, especially Zen Buddhism. In its quest for the essence of things and its flight from disorder, Zen philosophy is firmly rooted in the concept of minimalism. The Zen effort to eliminate everything superfluous, reaching a simplicity that allows greater concentration and deeper appreciation of everything that surrounds us, has turned into the minimalist dream of the twenty-first century.

The geometric style of Bauhaus-inspired
minimalism during the sixties and
seventies abandoned the aerodynamic
forms of the fifties.

The Zen lifestyle, the essence of which is reached when the unnecessary is eliminated, corresponds to the philosophy that permeates traditional Japanese houses. The austerity of these houses is not seen as deprivation, but rather as liberation of the inner being by banishing disorder, ostentation, and vanity from our environment.

This austerity is perhaps best expressed in the purest style of tea house architecture, whose construction methods, later extended to other types of buildings, gave rise to the important style known as *Sukiyazukuri*. However, the original approach claimed not to focus on the building materials but on the emptiness that they contained, resulting in the definition of tea houses as "houses of the soul" or "houses of emptiness." In fact, one can argue that this kind of architectural style, principally developed by Zen monks at the end of the sixteenth century, is the only philosophy before the arrival of the Modern Movement that rejects the incorporation of decorative elements, ostentation, and complexity in favor of simplicity.

The reason why one empty space works
and another does not could be a question
of a few inches in one direction or
another.

In the construction of tea houses, known as *chashitsu*, the form derived directly from the function (something that reminds us of one of the main postulates of functionalism). They were designed to unite a small group of people (a maximum of six) in a relaxed environment around a cup of tea, while fostering profound spiritual satisfaction through the acts of drinking tea and silent contemplation. Some Zen monks brought specific innovations to the tea ceremony. Among them is Rikyu (1522-91), considered to be the founder of the ceremony as it is practiced in Japan today. Rikyu thought that the proper spirit for the ceremony consisted of four elements: harmony, reverence, purity, and tranquility. He believed that, in general, man was too egotistical and worried about protecting himself from others and the world at large. For this reason, Rikyu wanted to create, through the art of tea, an atmosphere of such tranquility that men would feel no threat. Based on this tranquility, each person would obtain an intuitive sense of the harmony that can be found in nature and a purity of heart acquired by an understanding of this harmony. This purity would bestow upon the individual such a state of well-being as to result in respect for all of nature's creations. Consequently, the tea ceremony is a good way of escaping from the wrath and jealousy of everyday life, and from the need for self-defense, finally reaching the spirit that transcends the form. What is created in the *chashitsu* is a poem of eternity in the shape of a building.

"...Furniture, including the walls which
separate rooms, are not compact,
monumental, apparently or really fixed;
but they are vaporous pieces which
appear to have sprouted in the room,
as if someone had drawn them."

Marcel Breuer, 1928

Another surprising example of the effect of the empty spaciousness that infuses tea houses can be found in classic rock gardens, where the carefully composed stones underline absence. In both cases, the richness of the simplicity, the fascination for absence, and the respect for detail are evident. Minimalism is a resource at the disposal of today's society which allows us to get closer to this particular aesthetic, absorbing its capacity to find transcendence in simplicity.

To clarify this "transcendent simplicity," it is necessary to make clear another concept inherent in the Zen aesthetic: the words *sabi* and *wabi*. *Wabi* and *sabi* refer not only to the quest for the strictest or most "puritanical" simplicity, but also signify freedom from anger, envy and anxiety. *Wabi* can also be understood as an element of renunciation and welcome absence. When an interior is created with *wabi* and *sabi*, the inhabitant relates intimately with his environment, filling the empty spaces and finishing the composition in his mind, so it becomes a part of him and he a part of it.

■

"One explanation for the richness of
simplicity could be that architecture
which does not refer to anything outside
itself, which does not appeal to the
intellect, automatically gives priority to
direct experience, the sensory experience
of space, material and light."

Hans Ibelings

Some of history's most prominent modern architects such as Frank Lloyd Wright or Mies van der Rohe, found a clear source of inspiration in the concept of spaciousness developed by traditional Japanese architecture, or *sukiya-zukuri*. This vision conceptualizes space not as defined by walls and ceilings, but as something independent whose value is its own emptiness. Moreover, within Zen Buddhism, it is often said that the nature of all things is empty (*shunya*), but this emptiness (*shunyata*) is not the same as nothingness, because it designates the identity of everything. This kind of architectural expression and other forms of visual arts are not just a reflection of, but the material incarnation of, this spiritual emptiness that the Buddhists, and one might also dare to say the minimalists, want to reach.

Looking to Buddhist thinking, which has dominated Japanese thought for almost a thousand years, speaks to the need to find new means of expression that would introduce spirituality and calm into the frenetic and saturated style of contemporary Western life. Without achieving the austerity and extreme emptiness of traditional tea houses, we may try to remove all that is not necessary from our homes, and so attain the atmosphere of profound tranquility in the tea ceremony created by the master Rikyu; a state that can help us to learn more about ourselves and to feel in peace with the outside world. This results in interiors where we can enjoy the present, that transmit balance and order, that eliminate vanity through their simplicity, and that are lasting and eternal, resistant to the passing of different fashions and times.

"Cultural evolution is equivalent to the
elimination of ornaments from all
articles used on a daily basis."

Adolf Loos

Interiors & Colour: Concepts

Colour & Perception

One could say that colour is the essence of light and that light is the essence of life. Colour perception is a subjective experience, due to the fact that it isn't a material attribute, but a sensation produced by the reflection of light, transmitted to the brain by the eye. Thus, the colour of an object is the result of the change experienced by light when it is reflected, and white light, as we see it, is the integration of all the colours of the spectrum. If we see the colour white, this means that the material reflects all light. If we see a colour in particular, this means that its surface reflects the corresponding wavelengths for that colour and that it absorbs the rest. If we see black, then all the light is being absorbed.

The perception of colour provokes different reactions in each person, depending on a number of interrelated factors that are generally associated with cultural inheritance and experience. Among these factors, certain ones stand out: chromatic relations (the perception of a tone depends on its relationship with the surrounding tones); surface relations (the influence of the size of a coloured surface); texture; symbolic and cultural values; and optical effects (or chromatic illusions).

The relation of values, saturations and
the warmth or coldness of pure colours
can cause prominent differences in our
perception of colour.

The way in which a surface reflects, absorbs or transmits light and the way in which the colours and textures surrounding it influence its colour helps us to determine an object's shape and position. The same tone appearing on different surfaces or materials, such as metal, wood, cotton, velvet, linoleum, etc. can appear to be completely different. For example, a table lacquered in bright red will reflect light and its colour will be intensified while the same red on plain cloth will be comparatively duller.

On the other hand, as far as the symbolic value of colour is concerned, one of the most important attributes that affects the decoration of interiors is colour thermic sensation: some tones are perceived as warm (yellows, reds and oranges) and others as cold (blues, greens and violets). The temperature of the colour directly affects the perception of space in a room because it is thought that warm colours advance and move closer to the observer while cold colours recede and appear to move away.

■

"Objects, after postmodernism, will never
be as transparent as in the projects of
early industrial modernity, despite the
fact that they are as discreet as they
used to be. There must be something in
objects that invites us to reflect ourselves
in the sensory qualities of that which we
have before us."

Marcello Ziliani

Due to the phenomenon of colour temperatures, a red piece of furniture will be perceived as closer than a blue one, even if they are both situated at the same distance. For the same reason, a room with walls painted in a warm colour produces a cozy and enveloping sensation, but is visually weightier and makes one feel that the space is smaller. On the contrary, a room with walls painted in a cold colour (or one with low intensity or saturation) appears calmer and more spacious, although the atmosphere tends to seem colder. In general, the juxtaposition of cold and warm colours tends to intensify both of them. Colour can be used to alter the apparent proportions of a room; if we have a long narrow space, we can give the illusion of better proportions by painting the far wall in a darker colour. Similarly, in an excessively square room, we can reduce the effect by painting one of the walls a more intense colour than the other three.

Furthermore, both artificial and natural light have an effect on the perception of colour. For example, the warm light of an incandescent lightbulb intensifies yellows and reds, but diminishes the colder colours. Halogen strip lights produce a whiter and brighter light. Fluorescent lights intensify cold colours and diminish warm ones. The orientation of a room determines the quality of the natural light that it receives. Spaces that face north receive less direct light and tend to be colder, while rooms with southern exposure receive warmer light. Generally, in order to balance the colour temperature in the room, warm colours are used in rooms that face north while colder colours are used in rooms that face south.

Light and shade show the poetry of form,
just as the folds of a kimono reveal the
hidden positions of the body.

Another variable that influences the perception of colour is the relationship between figure and background. The relationship between an object and its environment relates to our tendency to select and order what we see, interpreting any shape as a figure against a background. In fact, there are people who feel disoriented in environments in which the relationship between detail and background is not obvious, such as rooms where the floor, furniture and walls are all of the same colour. From this we can deduce that when we enter a room, we perceive the different shapes that occupy the space based on the differences between their colours. Consequently, we can say that objects are primarily viewed as colours of different shapes and types.

Colour & Interaction

In order to produce colour, a simple base of three pigments is used, which when mixed together give a large number of intermediate tones. These are known as the **primary colours** – red, yellow and blue – on which all the other colours are based. When we mix two primaries, we obtain **secondary colours**: orange (yellow + red), green (yellow + blue), and violet (red + blue). The combination of a primary colour with one of its corresponding secondary colours results in one of the six **tertiary colours**.

■

"...to keep on designing furniture, objects
and articles for the home, is not the
solution to the problems of the house,
nor to those of life itself. No
embellishment is sufficient to remedy the
ravages of time, the errors of man, nor
the bestiality of architecture. The
solution consists of freeing oneself even
more of these design activities, perhaps
adopting the technique of a minimum
effort in a general process of reduction."

Superstudio design group

Colours are defined by three metric qualities: tone, value and saturation. These qualities allow us to order them by creating an identification system for the multiple chromatic variations possible. The *tone*, or shade, is the qualitative variation of the colour, and depends on the wavelength of its radiation; the human eye is capable of distinguishing 12,000 tones. Colours without tone are called achromatic or neutral colours, and are white, black and neutral grays. The *value*, or luminosity, is the quantity of light that a colour reflects; white is the colour that has the highest value. Each colour has different degrees of luminosity. The *saturation*, or intensity, is the degree to which a tone predominates. Consequently, a pale colour has little saturation while the primary colours are saturated to the max; the saturation can be varied by adding black or white so that the colour appears brighter or duller.

The **chromatic circle** is a visual system for ordering colours that takes the primary colours and their binary combinations as its base. This is particularly useful for decoration because it helps us to understand the relationships that exist between colours. Based on this, we can create colour schemes that are better adapted to each individual. In the circle, the complementary colour of each tone is directly opposite it.

"Their mass does not take
up any space."

*Marcel Breuer,
describing his steel tube chairs*

Chromatic relationships demonstrate that the perception of a tone is relative and depends on its relationship with the environment and other tones, which can significantly alter the appearance of the tones involved. In this comparison, the variables of tone, value and saturation are very important. With the chromatic circle, we can see that the most distinct tones are the complementary ones, between which there is a maximum degree of contrast that accentuates their differences. If, on the other hand, the tones are not significantly different, there is an affinity between them.

We can base our decorative criteria on different types of **colour combinations** in order to create harmonious atmospheres pleasing to the eye and showing an intrinsic sense of order positioned between boredom and chaos. Although there are no fixed rules, because harmony is the result of experimentation and a matter of personal taste, the main colour combinations are: monochromatic, based on value and saturation variations of a single colour; analogous, which combine colours close to each other on the colour wheel; and complementary, which are created from colours in opposing positions on the colour wheel.

■

"Pieces of furniture are not dead
objects, because they influence you in
subtle ways. Their particular qualities or
weaknesses will mark you for your whole
life: they will enlarge you or shrink you,
they will reward you or punish you,
in a definitive way."

Leon Krier

Colour & Psychology

The colour that we perceive around us not only provides us with objective information about the world, but also affects our sentiments and our emotional state. Reciprocally, the perception of colour is also affected by the influence of psychological and social factors, because we react to colour differently depending on who we are and what significance our culture gives to various colours. For this reason, the symbolic meaning of a colour may have very different connotations depending on the period or culture. In reality, giving meanings to colours is a tradition that is as old as humanity; for example, purple in the Roman Empire, blue in eighteenth-century Europe and yellow in Imperial China are colour variants attributed to royalty in different eras and cultures.

Humanity's need to develop colour symbolism is directly related to its need to experience the well-being that is produced by colour perception. In this sense, some believe that the human capacity to feel colour derives from our desire to obtain pleasure and from our need for survival.

Frank Lloyd Wright conceived a building
as a complete creation, where the
interior furniture would be in harmony
with the shape and materials
of the structure, created to be a
part of a specific
geographic location.

Goethe once said, "Colours act upon the soul. They can stimulate sensations, awaken emotions and ideas that calm us or excite us and provoke sadness or happiness." In other words, colour plays a fundamental role in the world in which we live and, consequently, in our lives as far as its capacity to affect our emotions and provoke reactions and sensations. Colour can animate or depress, stimulate or tranquilize, unify or divide, enlarge or diminish, invite conversation or disagreement, provoke interest or confusion, and it can contribute to the image we have of ourselves and those around us. For this reason, the choice of colour in the decoration of our homes should not be taken lightly, but should be done considering this series of conditioning elements.

In general terms, each of the colours of the spectrum is associated with specific **emotional effects,** which can be useful when choosing the colour of a wall or a piece of furniture.

Observing the effects that colours have
on each other is the starting point for
understanding the relativity of colour.

RED: Reddish tones generate a sensation of heat and tend to move closer to the observer due to the fact that they have a longer wavelength and consequently, a shorter focal point. On a symbolic level, red is associated with happiness and contentment, along with the heart, flesh, emotion and passion. An intense red makes the greatest emotional impact, but as it moves towards pink, it seems more relaxed, more friendly and more feminine. In decoration, bright red combines perfectly with neutral colours, such as white or black that accentuate its expressive strength even more, or with brownish tones.

ORANGE: In the words of Wassily Kandinsky, "Orange is red brought closer to humanity by yellow." It is an unmistakably warm colour, closely associated with autumn and the earth. It is stimulating, spiritually optimistic and generates energy and happiness. Psychologically, orange behaves in the same way as yellow: it is animated, expansive, rich and extroverted. It is a colour particularly oriented towards food and for this reason is often used in kitchens.

YELLOW: This colour is traditionally associated with intelligence. The colour of spring, the sun, light, intensity, happiness, yellow has ability to stimulate and animate; in its purest form it radiates heat and inspiration. Yellow is frequently used in children's rooms; in China, it has been venerated as a favorable colour since time immemorial.

■

Shubui, a fundamental part of Zen
philosophy, involves the strengthening
of self-discipline and the casting out
of everything which is not essential.

GREEN: The colour of life and of the silent power of nature, green's attributes include a relaxing effect and sedative properties and is related to the qualities of stability, security, and emotional balance. It is one of the most ambivalent colours of the spectrum and the one with the most opposing meanings: it is associated both with envy and with love, because it is the colour of Venus. There is an ancient belief that claims it has beneficial relaxing effects on the eyes.

BLUE: The colour of the spirit, of the sky, and of water, blue is related to characteristics of nobility. It has been classified as a cold colour and, in contrast to warm colours, it gives the sensation of distance owing to the fact that its wavelength is shorter which increases its focal point, making blue objects appear further away. Although it is fundamentally a healthy colour, at times it can signify melancholy or sadness. It is especially recommended for bedrooms or places of rest.

VIOLET: Born out of the union of opposites, violet absorbs the passion of red and the spirituality of blue. This contrast generates tonalities that can provoke both desire and aversion (this is what is known as "psychologically oscillating" tonality). Thus, combined with skill it evokes celestial delicacy or great richness but, if combined clumsily, gives a sense of decomposition. Violet is related to intimacy and sublimation and indicates profound sentiments. Violet light possesses the most energy, and it was not in vain that Claude Monet said "... finally, I have found the true colour of the atmosphere, it is violet. Fresh air is violet."

■

The ornament has no place in the Zen
tradition, because it comes from
the superficial and ostentatious
part of our minds.

Minimalism & Colour: Expressive Simplicity

Bearing in mind everything that has been covered so far, what does living in an environment built on the principles of minimalism, and on those of the perception and the psychology of colour, mean? Primarily, it answers some of the needs posed by today's society in industrialized countries. Secondarily, in relation to mankind's needs in particular, it means going beyond the strict and more austere minimalist approaches that were prevalent in interior design in the 1990s.

As far as an answer to the needs of society, minimalism is a philosophy that preaches a lifestyle based on simplicity, rejecting the uncontrolled consumerism promoted by the media. Applied as an answer to an internal need, and not as another fashion or stylistic trend, the creation of a vital environment based on simplicity could qualify as a revolution and a liberation.

"People are the measurement
for all furniture."

Friedrich Wilhelm Möller

Speaking in general terms, minimalism in decoration could be defined as a look towards the spontaneity of the present, as a free moment without historical burdens and worries about the future. The important thing, as highlighted by the postulates of the artistic movement and Zen Buddhism, is the immediate experience of the here and now. The goal is the naked beauty of the moment which finds maximum expressiveness in the least ornamentation possible. In fact, it is a complex process of liberating everything superfluous, a reaction to the current trend for accumulating unnecessary things which rapidly become obsolete. Minimalism is a return to authenticity, to the intrinsic quality of materials and textures, as opposed to the superficiality of useless objects.

The industrial concept of maximum
functionality drives the design of
minimalist kitchens, which seem to
gravitate around a nucleus, usually
tinted with colour.

Colour plays an essential role in creating more "human" environments that respond to the need to live surrounded by colour. The direct and unmistakable perceptions conveyed to us by the brushstrokes of colour contrast with minimalism's particular lightness of shapes and forms, which at times appear to be diluted in space. When minimalism and colour are united appropriately, and in just the right doses, the results are compositions that produce harmony derived from the order of the parts. In these interiors, it looks as if nothing could be added or removed, because everything fulfills a determined function. The position and proportion of different objects, of the empty spaces between them, and the distribution of colour appear interrelated and form a compact whole. The distribution of these objects and colours must achieve a dynamic composition that transmits some tension when viewed, in order to avoid the monotony or boredom caused by a too neutral interior. Shapes, colours, textures and light are resources that are capable of awakening centres of attention that, based on a certain asymmetry, generate movement.

■

"I think it's difficult to design a
'beautiful table': it depends not only on
the instruments used, but also on a
subtle, fragile uncertain wisdom.
A wisdom with which, at some point in
time, someone, who knows how and who
knows why, manages to channel in the
project of an event the total perception
of our cosmic adventure, even though it
might be provisional, suspended and
incomprehensible."

Ettore Sottsass

Minimalism implies an effort of reduction, which leaves only the indispensable, only the essence. Everything else is superfluous. And within this search for pure and naked geometric forms, colour plays a predominant role because of its undisputed descriptive capacity, and the narrative discourse that it transmits in an implicit, unconscious, connotative way. The introduction of vibrant colours in a room, whether through furniture or painted walls, adds touches of visual impact that, in addition to bringing life to the atmosphere break up the characteristic neutrality of the minimalist style. Even Zen defends the introduction of colour in interiors, because of its concentrated individuality and its specific attributes, like the properties that a spice can add to a dish.

In an ambience characterized by emphasis on the fluidity of light and space, the subtleties of colour take on special importance, showing the infinite effects produced by the variations of the textures. The effects that have the greatest impact are obtained by visually opposing textures and colours. By adding unexpected touches of brilliant or natural colours, the atmosphere is filled with new centres of attention, which personalize the aesthetic purity of the space. This is part of the evolution from the severest form of minimalism, correcting the error that is often made of identifying minimalism exclusively with the colour white, a similar mistake to considering emptiness to be a lack of content.

■

The warm colours par excellence are
yellow, orange and red. The latter is the
most intense, activating adrenaline more
than any other pure colour and
establishing a suitable ambience
for conversation.

The space, the materials and textures, and the light and the colours, become the fundamental elements that give significance to these interiors. The choice of colour is not at all fortuitous, because when so much depends on so little, each decision takes on a crucial importance. The different perspectives that we experience as we move around these environments allow us to appreciate the delicate harmony of the whole, in which the colours contribute different sensations according to their lighting and their relationship with the other elements of the room. In this way the emptiness is filled with content, establishing a balanced co-existence between simplification and the eloquence of colour, which enriches the sensory experience.

In these interiors, the "less is more" of Mies van der Rohe leads to ambiences which find their fulfillment in geometric simplicity, austerity of emptiness, the emotive capacity of colour and the dynamic force of the present. They replace the ornamentation of domestic space with a quest for maximum control over space. This has two direct consequences: on the one hand, the possibility of drawing a direct connecting line between architecture and interior decorating; on the other hand, the necessity to be honest with oneself by means of a not only aesthetic but moral conviction, given that the elimination of the distractions in traditional houses lays bare the imperfections, not only of the architecture, but also of the soul.

■

"The constant search for the archetypal
simplicity should justify, by itself, the
birth of a new object in our already
over-populated consumer society, without
adding gratuitous formal glitz introduced
in the project only to please the public."

Alberto Alessi

As an exercise in the simplification of the vital environment, minimalism is the effort of introspection, which helps us to determine what is really important. Applied to our society, this does not imply reaching the extreme of the total austerity of a Shaker community or a Zen monastery, but that each person must find the level of materialist reduction with which he or she feels comfortable. The main requirement is respect for space and for the subtleties of materials and details, learning to find beauty in the simplest of things. The fluidity of light through space, with its infinite play of light and shade, or the enormous impact that a colour exercises over the general appearance of a room, are examples of some of the subtleties laid bare by minimalist interiors.

"The designer's function should be that
of someone who observes how people live
and who can visualize the way in which
things can be improved."

Niels Diffrient

In an environment where visual, spatial and tactile sensations are central, and where every small detail is of essential importance, the effects that colours generate are essential to the achievement of a harmonious atmosphere. From the point of view of visual experience, harmony is understood as that which is pleasing to the eye. Consequently, an ambience where chromatic harmony reins creates an intrinsic sense of order and balance in the visual perception. When harmony is broken, the resulting whole transmits either chaos or boredom, depending on whether the stimulation is too strong or too weak. There are a multitude of possible chromatic schemes or combinations that generate changes in the dynamic balance of interiors. For example, a colour scheme based on the combination of complementary colours, like red and green, creates the maximum contrast and the maximum visual stability. Furthermore, if colours are applied correctly, sometimes audaciously, certain compositions can be obtained to achieve specific objectives. For example, to add depth to a room (like a white surface on a black wall), multiply the luminosity with intense touches of yellow. Or, to create shadowed areas, use the colour black, which absorbs light.

"It seems justified to affirm: the more
cultivated a people becomes, the more
decoration disappears."

Le Corbusier, 1925

In conclusion, we can state that the evolution of minimalism is supported by strong contrasts between the neutrality of light colours and the introduction of intense accents of colour. Also in this sense, it is necessary to exercise restraint and precision, which preserves the empty space. The combination of minimalism and colour should allow the final result to remain faithful to the minimalist principle of formal reduction, strengthening the capacity to get rid of everything that is not essential. Functionalism and simplicity should be the starting point when choosing furniture, textures, and colours, taking into account how they are interrelated. Thus the postulates of the strictest minimalism, whose extreme perfection and austerity gave rise on numerous occasions to houses more like an abode for the gods than habitable space for mere mortals, are humanized.

The concentration of mental energies
in the subtleties of proportion are
located at the very heart of the
minimalist mystery.

Minimalist interiors are therefore allied with the power of colour, becoming friendlier and more flexible. From the premise of eliminating disorder, confusion and the superfluous, as a way to regain form and a sense of our environment, interiors are reduced to the basic, becoming a universal style that everyone can enjoy. By showing the elements in the simplest and clearest way possible, an environment is created which appeals directly to the senses. As a philosophy aiming to improve society, minimalism establishes the guidelines to eliminate distractions and material things from the domestic environment, creating homes where people can find balance. This effort of simplification creates spaces with a wider margin of freedom, where the individual feels like the master of the habitable space, not like its servant.

"Whether people are conscious
of it or not, they currently obtain their
countenance and their sustenance from
the atmosphere of the things they live
with. They are rooted in them, just like
the plant is rooted in the earth."

Frank Lloyd Wright

furniture index

directory

ALNO UK
Unit 10
Hampton Farm Ind.Est.
Hampton Road West
Hanworth
Middlesex TW13 6DB
Tel. + 44 (0)20 8898 4781
Fax. + 49 (0)20 8898 0268
www.alno.co.uk
Contemporary kitchens

ARTEMIDE
Showroom
90–92 Great Portland Street
London W1W 7JY
Tel. + 44 (0)20 7631 5200
www.artemide.com
Contemporary light fittings

AXIA
Via delle Querce 9
31033 Castelfranco Veneto
Treviso
Italy
Tel. + 39 0423 496 222
Fax. + 39 0423 743 733
www.axiabath.it
*Contemporary bathrooms
and accessories*

B&B ITALIA
250 Brompton Road
London SW3 2AS
Tel. + 44 (0)20 7591 8111
www.bebitalia.co.uk
*Italian designed furniture
and interior accessories*

BELLATO
Via Azzi 36
31040 Castagnole di Paese (TV)
Italy
Tel. + 39 0422 438 800
Fax. + 39 0422 438 555
www.pallucobellato.com
*Designers, manufacturers and
distributors of original Italian
designed furniture*

BO CONCEPT
158 Tottenham Court Road
London W1T 7NH
Tel. + 44 (0)20 7388 2447
Fax. + 44 (0)20 7388 2448
www.boconcept.com
Furniture and interior accessories

CALLIGARIS
Viale Trieste 12
33044 Manzano
Udine
Italy
Tel. + 39 0432 748 211
Fax. + 39 0432 250 104
www.calligaris.it
Functional Italian designed furniture

CATTELAN ITALIA
Via Pilastri 15
36010 Carre' (Vi)
Italy
Tel. + 39 0445 318 711
Fax. + 39 0445 314 289
www.cattelanitalia.com
*Italian designed furniture and
home accessories*

CHARLES PAGE
61 Fairfax Road
London NW6 4EE
Tel. + 44 (0)20 7328 9851
www.charlespage.co.uk
Clean-lined designer furniture

CHRISTOPHER FARR
6 Burnsall Street
London SW3 3ZJ
Tel. + 44 (0)20 7349 0888
www.cfarr.co.uk
Contemporary collection of rugs

CLUB 8
at Christopher Pratts
9 Regent Street
Leeds LS2 7QN
Tel. + 44 (0)113 234 8000
Fax. + 44 (0)113 234 4404
www.@club8.com
Furniture and interior accessories

THE CONRAN SHOP
Michelin House
81 Fulham Road
London SW3 6RD
Tel. + 44 (0)20 7580 5333
www.conran.co.uk
*Furniture, lighting, homeware
and accessories*

CVO FIREVAULT
38 Great Titchfield Street
London W1W 8BQ
Tel. + 44 (0)20 7589 7401
Fax. + 44 (0)20 7255 2234
www.cvo.co.uk
*Contemporary and minimalist
fireplaces and home accessories*

FLOS
at McInnes Cook
31 Lisson Grove
London NW1 6UB
Tel. + 44 (0)20 7723 7005
www.flos.net
*Contemporary lighting including
outdoor lighting*

DORNBRACHT
Köbbingser Mühle 6
58640 Iserlohn
Germany
Tel. + 49 (0)2371 4330
Fax. + 49 (0)2371 433232
www.dornbracht.de
Modern bathrooms and accessories

FUSION GLASS DESIGNS
365 Clapham Road
London SW9 9BT
Tel. + 44 (0)20 7738 5888
www.fusionglass.co.uk
*Glass interior details, screens, stairs
and sculpture to commission*

GEOFFREY DRAYTON
85 Hampstead Road
London N1 2PL
Tel. + 44 (0)20 7387 5840
www.geoffrey-drayton.co.uk
Modern furniture and lighting

GIORGETTI
Via Montena Poleone 18
20121 Milan
Italy
Tel. + 39 0276 003 875
Fax. + 39 0276 000 136
www.giorgetti-spa.it
Designers of modern furniture

HABITAT
The Heals Building
196 Tottenham Court Road
London W1T 7LD
Tel. + 44 (0)20 7631 3880
and branches
www.habitat.net
*Furniture (including kitchen and
bathroom), lighting, homewares
and accessories*

HEALS
The Heals Building
196 Tottenham Court Road
London W1T 7LD
Tel. + 44 (0)20 7636 1666
www.heals.co.uk
*Furniture (including kitchen and
bathroom), lighting, homewares
and accessories*

INGO MAURER
Catalytico Ltd
25 Montpellier Street
London SW7 1HJ
Tel. + 44 (0)20 7225 1720
Fax. + 44 (0)20 7225 3740
www.ingo-maurer.com
Contemporary lights and lamps

JUVENTA
Slipstraat 4
8880 Ledegem
Belgium
Tel. + 32 56 50 01 91
Fax. + 32 56 50 39 37
www.juventa.be
Minimalist furniture

KEUCO GmbH
Postfach 1365
D-58653 Hemer
Germany
Tel. + 49 (0)2372 90 4-0
Fax. + 49 (0)2372 90 42 36
www.keuco.de
*Stainless steel and aluminium lighting,
home accessories, mirrors and storage*

KLENK COLLECTION
Industriestraße 34
72221 Haiterbach
Germany
Tel. + 49 (0) 7456 938 20
Fax. + 49 (0)7456 93 82 40
www.klenk-collection.com
Storage systems and solutions

LAGO srl
Via Morosini 22/24
35010 San Giogio in Bosco
Padova
Italy
Tel. + 39 0495 994 299
Fax.+ 39 0495 994 199
www.lago.it
Storage systems and furniture

LIVING SPACE
36 Cross Street
London N1 2BG
Tel. + 44 (0)20 7359 3950
www.intospace.co.uk
*Original, minimalist designed
furniture originals*

THE LONDON LIGHTING COMPANY
135 Fulham Road
London SW3 6RT
Tel. + 44 (0)20 7589 3612
*Wide selection of lights, lamps
and outdoor lighting*

MASON
70 North Street
Leeds LS2 7PN
Tel. + 44 (0)113 242 2434
www.masonfurniture.com
*Large contemporary furniture
showroom*

MATTEO GRASSI
Via Padre Rovanati 2
22066 Mariano Comense
Italy
Tel. + 39 0362 500 971
Fax.+ 39 0362 500 974
www.matteograssi.com
*Italian designed furniture
and accessories*

MAXALTO
at B&B Italia
250 Brompton Road
London SW3 2AS
Tel. + 44 (0)20 7591 8111
www.bebitalia.co.uk
*Italian designed furniture
and interior accessories*

MOBILEFFE
Via Ozanam 4
20031 Cesano Maderno
Milan
Italy
Tel. + 39 0362 502 212
www.mobileffe.com
*Contemporary furnishings for
bedrooms and living rooms*

MÖLLER DESIGN
Residenzstraße 16
32657 Lemgo
Germany
Tel. + 49 52 61 98 59 5
Fax.+ 49 52 61 89 21 8
www.moeller-design.de
Modern furniture and storage systems

MUJI
41 Carnaby Street
London W1V 1PD
Tel. + 44 (0)20 7287 7323
and branches
www.mujionline.com
*'no brand' Japanese homewares,
furniture and accessories*

NANI MARQUINA
Carrer Església 4-6, 3er D
08024 Barcelona
Spain
Tel. + 34 932 376 465
Fax.+ 34 932 175 774
www.nanimarquina.com
Carpets, rugs, cushions and blankets

PEROBELL
Avda. Arraona 23
08205 Sabadell (Barcelona)
Spain
Tel. + 34 937 457 900
Fax.+ 34 937 271 500
www.perobell.com
Contemporary chairs and sofas

POGGENPOHL
at CP Hart
Arch 1
Deansgate Locks
Manchester M1 5LH
Tel: +44 (0)161 214 7200
Fax: +44 (0)161 214 7201
www.cphart.co.uk
Contemporary kitchen design

POLIFORM
278 Kings Road
London SW3 5AW
Tel. + 44 (0)20 7368 7600
*Minimalist Italian designed furniture
and storage systems*

RAPSEL
at VOLA UK
Unit 12, Amptill Business Park
Station Road
Bedfordshire MK45 2QW
Tel. + 44 (0)1525 841155
Fax. + 44 (0)1525 841177
Designer bathrooms and accessories

RATTAN WOOD spa
Via S.Rocco 37
31010 Moriago (Treviso)
Italy
Tel. + 39 0438 966 307
Fax.+ 39 0438 966 413
www.rattanwood.it
*Contemporary furniture, fittings and
accessories for home and garden*

ROCHE BOBOIS
421–425 Finchley Road
London NW3 6HJ
Tel. + 44 (0)20 7431 1411
www.rochebobois.com
Designers of modern furniture

SCAVOLINI
Via Risara 60–70 / 74–78
61025 Monteabbate
Italy
Tel. + 39 0721 443 1
Fax.+ 39 0721 443 404
www.scavolini.com
Modern kitchen design

SKK
34 Lexington Street
London W1R 3HR
Tel. + 44 (0)20 7434 4095
*Lighting specialist including spots,
tracks, uplights and downlights*

TECTA
at Aram
110 Drury Lane
London WC2B 5SG
Tel. + 44 (0)20 7557 7557
www.tecta.de
Designer tables and chairs

TISETTANTA spa
Via Tofane, 37
20034 Giussano
Milan
Italy
Tel. + 39 03 623 191
www.tisettanta.it
*Home furnishings, accessories,
kitchens and storage systems*

VARENNA
at Poliform
278 Kings Road
London SW3 5AW
Tel. + 44 (0)20 7368 7600
Minimalist Italian kitchen designs

VIELER INTERNATIONAL
Breslauer Straße 34
D-58614 Iserlohn
Germany
Tel. + 49 (0) 2374/52-0
Fax.+ 49 (0) 2374 52268
www.vieler.net
*Contemporary designed metal door
handles, bathroom accessories and
storage systems*